France

Come on a journey of discovery

Linda Pickwell

QEB Publishing, Inc.

Copyright © QEB Publishing, Inc. 2004

Published in the United States by
QEB Publishing
23062 La Cadena Drive
Laguna Hills
Irvine
CA 92653

Library of Congress Control Number 2004101784

ISBN 1-59566-062-3

Written by Linda Pickwell
Designed by Starry Dog Books Ltd
Editor Christine Harvey
Map by PCGraphics (UK) Ltd

Creative Director Louise Morley
Editorial Manager Jean Coppendale

Picture credits

Key: t = top, b = bottom, m = middle, c = center,
l = left, r = right

Corbis /Marc Garanger 23,
Ecoscene /Kjell Sandved 5tr, /Papilio/R Pickett 6, /
Neeraj Mishra 10, 30tl, /Karl Ammann 11t, 30tr, /Sally
Morgan 15, 30br, /Luc Hosten 22,/Kjell Sandved 23tr,
/Papilio / Robert Gill 26, /Karl Ammann 27tr, /Luc
Hosten 28bl, / Stephen Coyne 29;
Getty Images Front Cover, / Jack Hollingsworth 4–5,
30bl, / Johnny Johnson 7, / K Begg 8-9, /9cr, /Art
Wolfe 11b, /Stan Osolinski 12–13, / Johan Elzenga 14,
/Pascal Crapet 16, / Johan Elzenga 17, / Harald
Sund 1, 18–19, /Daryl Balfour 20, / Renee Lynn 21, /
Tim Davis 23bl, /Gavriel Jecan 24bl, / Art Wolfe
24–25, /Douglas-Hamilton 28tr.

Printed and bound in China

The words in **bold**
are explained in the
Glossary on page 28.

Contents

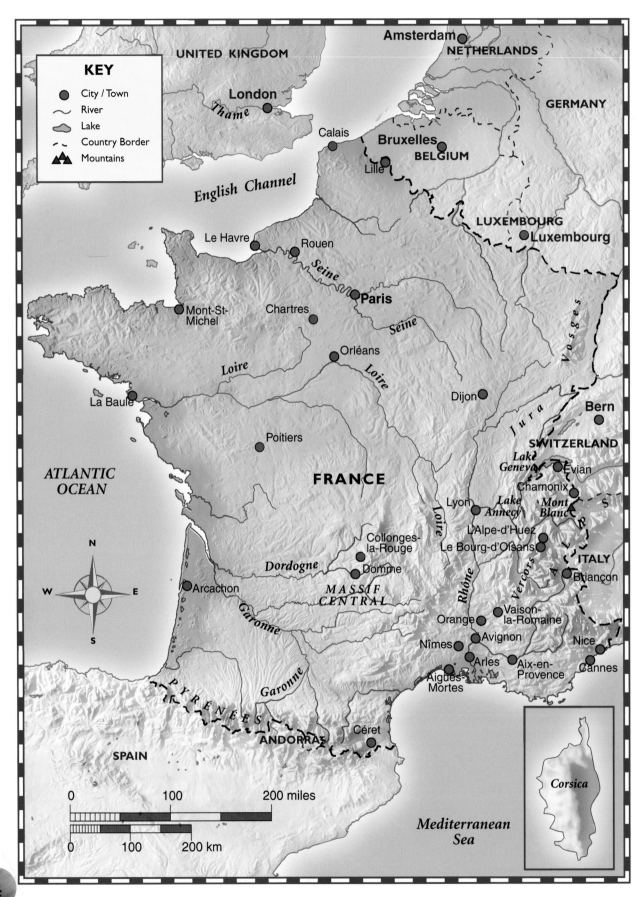

KEY

- ● City / Town
- ∿ River
- ⬭ Lake
- ┄ Country Border
- ▲ Mountains

UNITED KINGDOM

Amsterdam

NETHERLANDS

London

Thame

GERMANY

Calais

Bruxelles

BELGIUM

Lille

English Channel

LUXEMBOURG

Luxembourg

Le Havre

Rouen

Seine

Paris

Seine

Mont-St-Michel

Chartres

Orléans

Loire

Loire

Dijon

Vosges

La Baule

Jura

Bern

Poitiers

ATLANTIC OCEAN

SWITZERLAND

Lake Geneva

Evian

FRANCE

Chamonix

Lyon

Lake Annecy

Mont Blanc

N

W   E

S

Collonges-la-Rouge

L'Alpe-d'Huez

Le Bourg-d'Oisans

ITALY

Dordogne

Domme

Briançon

Arcachon

MASSIF CENTRAL

Vercors

Garonne

Orange

Vaison-la-Romaine

Nîmes

Avignon

Nice

Arles

Aix-en-Provence

Cannes

Garonne

Aigues-Mortes

PYRÉNÉES

ANDORRA

Céret

SPAIN

Mediterranean Sea

0   100   200 miles

0   100   200 km

Corsica

4

Where in the world is France?

France lies on the continent of Europe. It is the largest country in western Europe. France is surrounded by the countries Belgium and Luxembourg to the north, Germany, Switzerland, and Italy to the east, Spain to the south, and Britain lies to the northwest, across the English Channel.

Corsica is a French island located in the Mediterranean Sea, just off the northwest coast of Italy. It is over 100 miles long and covered by mountains.

France is largely a **rural** country with a fairly even spread of population. But it has many big cities and **urban** areas, too.

▼ France and its place in the world.

France

The national flag of France.

Did you know?

Name: **Republic** of France

Location Europe

Surrounding countries Belgium, Luxembourg, Germany, Switzerland, Italy, and Spain

Surrounding seas and oceans English Channel, Atlantic Ocean, Mediterranean Sea

Length of coastline 2,142 miles

Capital Paris

Area 211,207 square miles

Population 59,039,700

Life expectancy Male 73, Female 81

Religion Roman Catholic

Language French

Climate Moderate, combining Atlantic, Mediterranean, and continental influences

Highest mountain range Mont Blanc (15,770 feet)

Major rivers Loire (length: 630 miles), Seine (length: 488 miles), Rhône (length: 508 miles in total, 324 miles in France) and Dordogne (length: 294 miles)

Currency Euros (previously Francs)

What is France like?

A country of contrasts

France is a country of many contrasts, with coastal areas, flat agricultural **plains**, rivers, and lakes, and dramatic mountainous areas. It is divided into regions called *pays*, and each region has its own identity.

Traveling through the regions

As you travel southward through France, you will notice changes between regions in the way the land is used and the different styles of houses. In Brittany, the roofs of houses are made of silver-gray slate, while in Provence the houses are made of stone and have red terra cotta roof tiles.

Regional specialities

The regions are also known for their specialities. The Loire Valley is a great **horticultural** area. The Dordogne has small farms growing vegetables, almonds, walnuts, and fruit trees. The Auvergne and Burgundy have large areas of **vineyards** used in the wine industry.

Traveling along the coast

The Mediterranean Sea borders the southeast coast of France. This coastline has many sandy beaches

▲ Mont-Saint-Michel is a fortified abbey on the northern coast of France, near the border of Brittany and Normandy. It has two large towers to defend the entrance.

with hills behind, and is a major vacation destination.
It includes the Riviera and the Côte d'Azur.
  To the west is the Atlantic coast, which stretches from southern France to Brittany in the north.

▼ A popular beach at Antibes on the Mediterranean coast.

▼ The pretty, historic town of Dinan in Brittany.

My name is Christophe. I live on a farm in the Normandy region of France. We grow a lot of apples that are used to make apple juice and cider. After school and at weekends I help my father. The apples are pressed and the juice collected. Then it is stored for various lengths of time to make different types of cider.

  In the south are sandy beaches backed by sand **dunes**. As a result of the long stretch of coastline and the winds, there are often big waves.
  The Normandy coast, bordering the English Channel, has beaches and chalk cliffs. These were used for the D-Day landings during World War II.

Climate — traveling through the regions

Climate changes

As you travel through France you will notice that the climate varies from region to region. Temperatures are generally lower toward the north of the country.

The Atlantic regions

These lie in the northwest, and include regions such as Brittany. The weather can be mild, but sometimes it can be cold and damp. Brest has an average temperature of 42°F in January and 60°F in July, with moderate rainfall.

The continental regions

These lie in the northeast of France. Strasbourg has the most wide-ranging temperatures in France. In winter it is cold, with an average of 83 days of frost and snow. The summer rainfall often comes with fierce storms.

In winter a northerly wind blows down the Rhône valley. This is known as the *mistral*. You will most likely feel that it is an unusually cold and strong wind. It can blow at considerable speeds— more than 60 miles per hour. The mistral can flatten crops and cause damage to buildings.

The Mediterranean regions

These regions lie in the southeast of France. The warm Mediterranean Sea keeps the winters mild, with an average temperature of 46°F. The summers are hot, with temperatures over 85°F. Often it is so dry along the Mediterranean coast that forest fires break out.

◀ Forest fires can cause a huge amount of damage. They are a serious hazard in the south during the dry summer months.

My name is Claire. I live near Aix-en-Provence in the south of France. Last summer there were forest fires near here. We could see the smoke from our house and I was really frightened. The fires are often started by people who are careless with matches, and during the summer there are constant warnings about this. Whenever there is a fire my father is called to help because he works as a part-time firefighter.

▼ The ancient city of Strasbourg has a cathedral and many historic buildings.

Traveling through the mountains

The Alps

The largest mountain system in Europe is the Alps. Only part of the range is in France. They lie in the south east of the country and stretch 175 miles north to south and 80 miles east to west. The highest summit is Mont Blanc.

There is a road system through the French Alps that begins at Evian and finishes in Nice. This is a major tourist area for snow sports and climbing, walking, and sightseeing.

Beech and oak trees grow on the lower slopes, and fir and pine trees on the upper slopes. High in the mountains you can sometimes see chamois, which are like small, dainty antelope, and the ibex, a rare wild goat.

The Pyrenees

The mountain range called the Pyrenees forms the border between France and Spain. These mountains stretch for 250 miles. In total there are almost 13 square miles of **glaciers** within this range.

The Massif Central

This is a mountain range in south-central France. The Auvergne is the main part of this range. It has a dramatic volcanic landscape of domes and valleys created during volcanic eruptions many thousands of years ago. Lakes have formed in the empty craters that were once the center of the volcanoes.

My name is Chloe. I live in Chamonix in the Alps. Each day my mom travels to work in the café at the top of Aiguille du Midi, which is a pointed rocky summit that attracts a lot of tourists. She uses two cable cars to get from the bottom to just beneath the summit. Visitors reach the top by an elevator, built inside the snow-covered mountain.

▲ Ibex are excellent climbers and can leap easily across narrow, rocky ledges.

▶ At 15,770 feet, Mont Blanc is the highest mountain in western Europe.

Traveling along the River Seine

The river's source

The Seine begins life in northeast France, near Dijon. It flows through Paris before eventually reaching the English Channel at Le Havre, 235 miles from its **source**.

Paris

The River Seine runs through the center of Paris, splitting the city into two halves. The river is crossed by thirty-two bridges, some of which are more than 300 years old. The Notre Dame cathedral stands on the Île de la Cité (Island of the City) in the Seine. It is reached by bridges over the river.

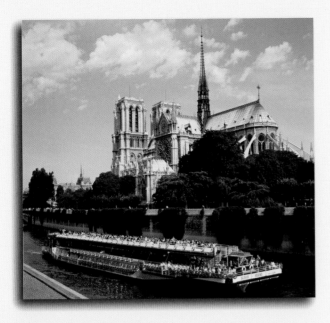

▲ A riverboat cruise along the River Seine gives the tourists a close-up view of Notre Dame cathedral.

Riverboat cruises are a very popular way for tourists and French children to go sightseeing in the capital city. Usually there is a guide on board who tells the passengers all about the historic sights along the way. There are also evening cruises.

Using the river for transport

The Seine is also used by boats to transport goods. Petroleum and building materials are the main cargo. Rouen, one of the many cities on the Seine, is a major port for large ships.

▼ The River Seine is the main commercial waterway of Paris.

Did You Know?

At 488 miles, the River Seine is the second longest river in France.

The worst flood of the River Seine was in 1910 when the river rose by 23 feet.

◄ Pont Neuf is the oldest of the thirty-two bridges on the Seine. It was built in the sixteenth century.

A trip to Paris

Steve and Amy live in New York and they are going to visit Paris with their parents. Their mom helped them find some information about Paris on the Internet before they went.

The capital city

They read that Paris is the capital city of France. It is famous for high-quality goods in the fashion and perfume industries. Paris also has many hotels and street cafés. It is a popular tourist attraction and this is a major source of income for the city and the country.

Transport

Steve and Amy also found out about the different ways of getting around Paris. There are two airports, Charles de Gaulle and Orly. Paris has rail links to forty-five cities in France and to many others in Europe. The railway system includes high-speed trains known as *TGV*, and there is a direct link with London, England, via the **Channel Tunnel**.

Paris has its own underground railway system called the Le Métro, which serves workers who commute into the city. The road that circles Paris is known as the *peripherique*.

▼ Beneath the Arc de Triomphe is the tomb of the unknown soldier, dedicated to fallen heroes.

These are some of the places that Steve and Amy visited in Paris. They wrote down some historical facts they discovered about each one in their notebooks.

► THE LOUVRE
This was once a royal palace. It became Europe's first museum in 1793. Now it is a famous art gallery where the **Mona Lisa**, painted by Leonardo da Vinci, is kept.

► THE EIFFEL TOWER
The tower was built in 1891. It is 1,050 feet high. It was designed by Gustave Eiffel. It is made of open-lattice wrought iron.

▼NOTRE DAME CATHEDRAL
This famous cathedral is over 800 years old. The building dates from 1163, when it was begun by Maurice du Sully. It is featured in the story "The Hunchback of Notre Dame" by Alexander Dumas.

◄ ARC DE TRIOMPHE
The arch was built in 1836 to celebrate Napoleon's victories. Twelve avenues lead from it, the most famous is the Champs Elysées.

► Some of the world's most famous gargoyles can be seen at Notre Dame cathedral.

Traveling through France

Each year many people visit France, traveling through the country to the south and the Mediterranean coast. If you come to France via England, the shortest ferry crossing is from Dover to Calais in France.

▼ The historic town of Calais is one of the busiest passenger and vehicle ferry ports.

Fontainebleu

Used as early as the twelfth century by French kings, who often went hunting for wild boar, Fontainebleau is a huge area of forest. It is famous today for its footpaths and wildlife, as well as for the palace, dating from 1528. Our journey continues south through vast agricultural areas, with fields of grain and crops, such as mustard and sunflowers.

▼ Sunflowers are widely grown in France. The oil from their seeds is used in cooking.

Calais

More passengers are handled in Calais than in any other French port. It was originally a small fishing port, but Calais is now a major transportation center for traffic to and from Europe. From Calais, we travel around the outside of Paris and soon reach historic Fontainebleau.

Dijon

The road continues to Dijon in central eastern France. This city is known for producing mustard and lace and has many old buildings, including the palace of the Dukes of Burgundy.

Lyon

We now travel on toward Lyon, passing many vineyards growing grapes for the production of wines. Lyon is the second most important city in France after Paris. It is a big commercial area with lots of different industries. The wide River Rhône runs through its center.

▼ As you travel through France you will see many historic buildings and bridges in this pale gold color stone.

Avignon

We continue to the historic town of Avignon, which is a center of culture. Each summer, visitors can see plays known as *son et lumière* (sound and light), which tell the story of the history of the town and the surrounding area.

South of France

South of Avignon we could travel anywhere on the Mediterranean coast, from Perpignan to Cannes, or Nice. Each year, in May, Cannes hosts the famous Film Festival, an important occasion for the international movie industry, which attracts thousands of visitors.

▶ With its warm Mediterranean sea and sunny climate, the French Riviera is a popular summer holiday destination.

Festivals and celebrations

A national celebration

If you were in France on July 14, you could join the special celebrations and national holiday of Bastille Day. This day marks the storming of the Bastille prison in 1789, when ordinary people forced open the prison in Paris. This uprising of the people is said to have started the French Revolution.

▼ Locals in costume and tourists enjoy a wine festival in Dijon.

Regional celebrations

When traveling around France you will come across traditional celebrations that have survived through the ages in most regions. Many of these have either a religious connection, or are held to celebrate food or drink. Often a village will hold a fête dedicated to a local food, such as a particular cheese or sausage.

Natalie and Pierre have written below about their local festivals.

In Vittel in eastern France, for example, there is a celebration at the end of April for tasting frogs legs, called *La Foire aux Grenouilles*.

Some places might celebrate a skill, such as lace-making or music. The city of Arles in Provence has a folk festival each year—the Festival of the Queen of Arles. People from all over the region come together in the traditional costumes of their area and celebrate in song and dance.

▲ Traditional Breton costume

Natalie lives in Bretagne (Brittany).
People here wear Breton costumes on special occasions and feast days. Women and girls wear embroidered dresses and headdresses made of stiffened lace. My mom and I both have traditional costumes. I love wearing mine and having my photograph taken by the tourists.

▼ Women singers at the Festival of the Queen of Arles in Provence

Pierre lives in Dijon.
Every year there is a folklore festival here. The men wear traditional wide-brimmed hats and the women wear full skirts, an apron, and a special headdress. I have a hat like dad's and I really like taking part in the celebrations.

Food and drink

The French are known to enjoy good food and wine. Many of the foods that are traditional in France have become well known in other countries.

Breakfast
Children will usually begin the day with a traditional French breakfast of **croissant**, **pain au chocolat**, or a **baguette** and jam. In rural areas ham or cheese may be added. Breakfast is usually served with hot chocolate or coffee.

Regional foods
Bread is eaten with most meals, and each region has its own favorites. There are many cheeses from the different regions, too, which are also popular in other countries. These include brie, goats' cheese, Cantal, and Camembert.

▼ Large areas of France are used to grow grapes for wine-making.

Wine
France is famous for the wines it produces. These include sparkling champagne and white and red wine. Wine is made from the juice of grapes that grow on **vines**. The vines grow best in the warm, dry parts of France such as Bordeaux and Burgundy.

▼ All the family helps to harvest the grapes for wine-making.

Crêpes are very popular in France. These are like pancakes but they are lighter and thinner. You will need an adult to help you make the crêpes.

Recipe for sweet crêpes

3 eggs
1/4 cup superfine sugar
1 3/4 cup flour
pinch of salt
2 teaspoons of melted butter or oil
1 pint milk

Beat the eggs and add the sugar, flour, salt, and butter or oil. Slowly add the milk and beat the mixture until smooth. Leave for one hour. Heat a small skillet. Pour in a small amount of the mixture. Turn or toss during cooking until golden on each side. Eat with a filling of your choice.

▲ A sweet crêpe

Our names are Sophie and Françoise. We are sisters. We help our parents in the vineyard, especially at harvest time. Some of the grapes are harvested by machine, but the vines on the steep slopes have to be picked by hand. There is a label with the name of the vineyard on it, and this is put on all of the bottles filled with the wine made here.

Energy and industry

Making electricity

Coal is not an important energy source in France any more. Most of the country's electricity is produced by nuclear power. So much electricity is produced that France now sells it to Britain, Italy, Germany, and the Netherlands.

Hydroelectric power

Many powerful rivers and waterfalls in the mountain areas of France have been used to provide hydroelectric power. Hydroelectric power stations can be found along the River Rhine, the River Rhône, in the Massif Central, and the Alps. About a quarter of the power for France is produced this way.

Often, huge dams are constructed across valleys. The River Rhône is crossed by eighteen dams and by thirteen power stations.

Modern industries

France produces iron and steel, tires, and parts for airplanes. Many cars are built in France, such as Renault, Citroën, and Peugeot. These are exported internationally.

Paris is the manufacturing center of the country. It is the international center for the fashion and perfume industries. Many famous stores attract customers from other countries.

▶ A hydroelectric dam on the River Loire.

Many people in France work in the tourist industry. The money that tourists spend helps bring in a huge income for the French economy.

Traditional industries

Farming is still important in France. There are large areas of **arable** land where wheat, barley, rice, and many sorts of vegetables and fruit are grown. Apples and grapes are important crops. Flowers are grown in the south for the perfume industry.

Huge areas of forest provide lumber. Cattle, sheep, pigs, and goats are kept for dairy products, and for meat, leather, and wool. Large fishing fleets work from ports in Brittany and on the west coast.

▶ Ten percent of French people work in the car industry.

The lives of two French children

▶ The historic town of La Rochelle is an important fishing port.

Arnaud

Arnaud lives in a village called Saint Veran in the Alps. It is the highest community in Europe. Arnaud's family make their living from farming, and grazing goats and sheep on the pastures. Arnaud helps out when he is not at school.

Arnaud's school is small and is in the next village. In the winter months he sometimes has to study at home, because the weather can prevent him from traveling. Arnaud spends his spare time outside with his friends. He learned to ski when he was very young. He enjoys riding his mountain bike in the summer. He would like to ride in the famous Tour de France race, in which the world's best bicyclists race around the country.

Benjamin

Benjamin lives in a town called La Rochelle on the Atlantic coast in western France. His father owns a seafood restaurant on the oceanfront, and many tourists and local people enjoy eating there.

Benjamin likes his town because it is next to the ocean. His father owns a yacht, which has sails and a motor. As much as possible Benjamin goes sailing with his father along the coast to visit other towns, such as Royan and St. Trojan.

Benjamin goes to the local school, which is a ten-minute walk from his home. After school he and his friends often swim in the sea or play **boules**.

▲ Children who live in the Alps learn to ski when they are very young.

▼ Riders in The Tour de France cycle race work hard to climb the mountain roads.

Arnaud wrote in his diary about the Tour de France

We had difficulty finding any space to stand at the roadside. People wrote the names of their favorite bicyclists on the road. At last, the bicyclists came and I could see how hard it was for them to race up the steep hill. I shouted my hero's name as loudly as I could when he rode past!

25

France's theme parks

Traveling to Disneyland Paris

This amusement park is around 25 miles east of Paris, at Marne-la-Vallée. It is an extension of the popular Disneyland in Florida. It has become known as "EuroDisney".

EuroDisney has forty-three attractions, which are built into five themed lands. For example, there is Frontierland, where there are shoot-outs between cowboys and Indians, and Fantasyland, where there are characters from stories such as "Sleeping Beauty." The complex also has other facilities, including themed hotels with a total of 5,800 rooms. The park has become one of the most visited tourist attractions in France.

Traveling to Parc Astérix

This amusement park is based on the French cartoon character Asterix the Gaul. It is 22 miles north of Paris. It was built in 1989.

When you arrive at the park you will see Druid stones, medieval villages, Roman soldiers, and a collection of Gauls, including Asterix, Obelix, and Unhygienix.

There are plenty of things to do at the amusement park. In addition to lots of rides, there are workshops where you will be able to make a Greek mask or a Roman necklace.

Steve and Amy visited Parc Astérix during their trip to Paris. Steve wrote a postcard to his Grandma.

Dear Grandma,
We came to Parc Astérix today. I was really excited as I'd been given an Astérix book for my birthday and wanted to see the characters in the park. I went on lots of rides and made a mask. I bought another Astérix book too!

love, Steve
x

Mrs. N. Wilkins
4 Hope Drive,
Wayne,
PA 19087
U.S.A.

Glossary

arable
land suitable for growing crops

baguette
a long, crusty stick of bread

boules
a ballgame played with metal balls and also called *pétanque*

Channel Tunnel
a tunnel under the English Channel that connects France and England

croissant
a crescent-shaped twist of flaky pastry traditionally eaten at breakfast

dunes
mound or ridge of loose sand

glacier
a very slow-moving river of ice

horticultural
growing crops and other produce

Mona Lisa
a painting by Leonardo da Vinci found in the Louvre in Paris

pain au chocolat
"chocolate bread," similar to a croissant with chocolate in the center

plains
large areas of flat land

republic
a country ruled by a government only

rural
about farming and the countryside

source
the start or place from which something begins

TGV
stands for *train à grande vitesse*, which means a very fast train

urban
living or situated in a town or city

vines
the plants which produce the grapes used for wine-making

vineyard
fields where grapes are grown for making wine

Index

Teaching ideas and activities for children

The *Travel Through* series of books offers up-to-date information and interdisciplinary opportunities for geography, English, math, history, religious studies, and citizenship. The series enables children to develop an overview ("the big picture") of each country. This overview reflects the huge diversity and richness of the life and culture of each country. The series aims to prevent the development of misconceptions, stereotypical images, and prejudices, which often develop when the focus of a study narrows too quickly onto a small locality within a country. The books in the series help children gain access to this overview and also develop an understanding of the interconnectedness of places. They contribute to the children's geographical knowledge, skills, and understanding, and help them to make sense of the world around them.

The following activities promote thinking skills and creativity. The activities in section A have been devised to help children develop higher-order thinking, while the activities in section B have been devised to promote different types of learning styles.

A: ACTIVITIES TO DEVELOP THINKING SKILLS
ACTIVITIES TO PROMOTE RESEARCH AND RECALL OF FACTS
Ask the child to:
- make a sketch of France to show the capital and the major cities, the main rivers, mountain ranges, and surrounding seas and oceans.
- research and investigate a mountain environment, such as the Alps or Pyrenees. The children can present their findings in a style of their choice.

ACTIVITIES TO PROMOTE UNDERSTANDING

Ask the child to:

• describe the regions and how the climate changes as you travel around France.

• investigate French cooking and to find a recipe to describe or make.

ACTIVITIES TO USE INFORMATION TO SOLVE PROBLEMS

Ask the child to:

• create a menu for a typical French meal.

• draw a sequence of diagrams to explain the growing of sunflowers.

ACTIVITIES TO ENCOURAGE ANALYTICAL THINKING

Ask the child to:

• compare and contrast life in the countryside with life in a city, such as Paris.

• discuss the various means of transportation by which they could travel to France and across the country.

• find out about the Roman settlements in France and how the Romans traveled from one to another.

ACTIVITIES TO STIMULATE CREATIVITY

Ask the child to:

• develop a dance based on the course of the River Seine. They could show a small stream growing to a slow-moving wide river and flowing into the ocean, or depict the life of Paris as the river passes through it.

• research geographical terms, using the Glossary in this book and other sources.

ACTIVITIES TO HELP CHILDREN USE EVIDENCE TO FORM OPINIONS AND EVALUATE CONSEQUENCES OF DECISIONS

Ask the child to:

• consider the values and concerns tourism brings to coastal or mountain regions.

• discuss when a mountain rescue team should try a rescue and whether there is a time when they should not. What are the consequences for both decisions?

B: ACTIVITIES BASED ON DIFFERENT LEARNING STYLES
ACTIVITIES FOR LINGUISTIC LEARNERS

Ask the child to:

• write instructions for a person making a crêpe.

• write a poem to illustrate a mountain range.

ACTIVITIES FOR LOGICAL AND MATHEMATICAL LEARNERS

Ask the child to:

• use a "living graph" to explain "A year in the life of a vineyard."
• create a "consequence wheel" about what would happen if the Seine flooded.

ACTIVITIES FOR VISUAL LEARNERS

Ask the child to:

• design a poster or comic strip to show what any aspect of French life is like.
• make a representation of any landscapes in France through collage.
• create a piece of artwork to illustrate the enormity of the mountains or glaciers.

ACTIVITIES FOR KINESTHETIC LEARNERS

Ask the child to:

• make a model of a structure based on the Eiffel tower.

ACTIVITIES FOR MUSICAL LEARNERS

Ask the child to:

• compose a song, rap or instrumental piece to celebrate a successful harvest.
• learn to sing a simple French song.

ACTIVITIES FOR INTERPERSONAL LEARNERS

Ask the child to:

• work in a group to develop a presentation about one aspect of France.
• work with others to produce a short sketch depicting a mountain rescue, a visit to a café, a lost child in Paris, or a trip up the Eiffel tower.

ACTIVITIES FOR INTRAPERSONAL LEARNERS

Ask the child to:

• say how they would feel if they were lost in Paris. How would they cope?
• look at photographs of different areas of France and choose the area they prefer, giving reasons.

ACTIVITIES FOR NATURALISTIC LEARNERS

Ask the child to:

• make notes about the effect of tourism on a specific area.
• prepare an argument, either for increasing tourism or limiting tourism.